The Pirates of Pen's Chance

the Pirates of Pen's Chance

Homolinguistic Translations
by
Douglas Barbour & Stephen Scobie

THE COACH HOUSE PRESS
TORONTO

DEDICATION

hiss of the mist on
a greater darkness

introducing the prince
who drives from the east
to the north, to the bard
that is

my favourite on the wing
pearl of great price
flowering high

equal portions of
the close embrace
be our garden

Contents

Minimal Lists

Agricultural Implement

like a dress, the fertile earth
dives into language

sterile beneath your feet, a breath
and a consonant shot

lounging in front of the palace
standing there blind

on the team with good muscles
scared to report

2.

seeing only makes us curious
how deeply each poem
extends: no data surfaces

unwanted penalty of notoriety:
agonised readers everywhere
dying, withering, halting

Edmonton's earnest librarians
blind and rational, read on:
we gesticulate, livid as zealots

eager didactic widows in their heat
rant and inquire numbers
with a telephone, endlessly

risqué bedroom episodes – infamous! –
deliver esoteric thrills: helpless,
enervated writers hope it talks

encyclopaedic charladies have insight
caution kills eroticism
nostalgia sickens

Lament for the Edmonton Eskimos

here heroes are chosen for winter
the actors find themselves acted

ashamed and naked all
disguises denied them
beneath the penalty of figures
the final grouping
before the age of heroes
was even conceived

madness will live forever
in names reversed by winter
washed to the outer edges
of the stories we tell today

●

and here we come to duality
the limited value
of what can be repeated
'let me recite what history teaches
history teaches'
the truth is changeable
and angrily they hurry
off in the wrong direction
not even half way there

composition by field
determines the need to be
decisive : what can be held
cuts deep

there is always another
question : you can't
afford to look back
poetry becomes commercial
that's what you said
on the weekend
that's what you used to say
most of the time

it just goes on and on
like a horror movie

the final question is one of temperature

Spring Song

Make when
When all and to
make when

Take count
Send then and
flower with

set of breast
Raucous
every making loose of

shrilling in fife
All with making
shrilling in

Make when
tawny bright-eyes gnarl
whiskey-jack make when

Make like
it swells fixed
Make like

Give through clod
things with
for only through

Make when fashion
garden hyacinth make
when

Let when rills
goldenwing icy
where let when

till long like this
some just waking
when

For when
strong vasts
so the joy till

Make from scraps
home-brought faded shreds
hues in

Let indolence
not let
Well let indolence

Give the all
at from
Give the

Only when make
Make cup
Make when

Speaking Spring

Saying only
           naturally green
saying that
         oh
saying

please renew instantly
now grow beyond yesterday

do it
and never ending
do it please

return in majestic
ascension

Western Landscapes

Western landscapes: the prairie, the
wind, the long line of horizon — smudged
when dust begins to rise: it takes
will power, stubborn determination,
thousands of back-breaking hours, and still those winds
blow fields and livelihood away, it is
the drought, the depression, all over again —
small crops and smaller harvests, praying for
rain before it's too late, before everything tumbles
down: the house, the mortgage, the barn, rattling like an old tin
can kicked down the highway — all for lack of
rain, oh sweetly suffering
Christ, of rain.
If this is the promised land, the last best west,
my outhouse is the Ritz. There isn't much to
love out here, remembering how things
were and will be again: you just have to dig yourself
in, into the soil, into the land, into the history,
my friend, the goddamn history — Riel taking up
arms, and Aberhart taking up votes,
and Lougheed now doing what
I don't know, it never ends, out here
in the West there's always a desperation, and
my heart goes out to it, down to it, oil and stone,
bed-rock, soil, the dust-devils blowing
again, in the 80s, again.

Fool's Song

                I was
                        the wind
        A foolish thing was
            the rain

                I came to
                        the wind
                                        men shut

            the rain

            when I came
                        the wind
            swaggering   never
                        raineth

                                my beds
                        the wind
        With tosspots
                rain   raineth

                        the world
                        the wind   the rain
            's all one
                                    every day.

Tempest Tossed

Idiot! don't you understand
how deep, how far down,
how immersed in the sea
thirty feet from the light of the sun,
your lover's superfluous body
is being eaten away
to a skeleton's virginal song?

Love is a dangerous flower, attended
by rodents, wolves, and winter;
like passing fashions at dawn
the iron of the sword is broken,
and songs of praise shift key
when sung by two cracked voices.

Meanwhile the highway's angel watches
the wanton hands of the clock,
cold as an east coast wind,
circling the grateful bird:

listen in dreams
to its chime of existence,
so dearly bought.

Anger Song No. 1

With no warning, the night for
Annie descends. It's like a song, the melody
gone, the words fading in memory, &
whose ideas of lust are we speaking of anyway. Her
eyes shone once, that's how a Romantic songwriter would put it,
to say nothing of her lovers, who all
compare them
with stars of course,
the night bright with radiance till
morning whitens the sky & the
sun rises like desire once again. Oh god!
not another sexual cliché
that misses the point, misses Annie completely.
I dont understand:
did no one notice Annie disappear?
Compare her life not her eyes I say
but those guys wont listen to me
I could as easily be on TV, the sound off, what
do I have to tell them anyway. I could
compare them with something, but for
now I'll just suggest
that they dont really care about her at all.
She's not really the image they seek, she's simply
gone, & good luck to her. She deserves some.

Money & Pain / Money & Pain

a word a synthesizer
conjunctives full of gold all gone

in a fog you flipt pages of light
an instrument controld by nightmare
a musical failure

clarinetists play precisely legal
poets in orgasm lose the prime avenger
only heaven allows why

french or english useless masses
of pedestrians still take orders from a wrestler

on the other hand
i can work things out
& tho no mathematician
philosopher of suffering only
i can still read a pair of scales

yr shitty wealth on one side
everyone else's hunger on the other

The Hudson Institute Predicts

by god she
sure looks tough

too bad about the kid tho
no future in foreign bank accounts

Once upon a

time threw people
were you hanging so proud
scrounging?

lonely you taught
you compromise mystery
selling his deal

jugglers' tricks, good people
chrome cat discover
it's everything

princess made precious ring
amused language
now nothing invisible

feel your direction
unknown stone

Anger Song No. 2

When everything meshes perfectly, it's
lovely interaction, soft generation of liquid vowels, consonance:
woman & man together. Together. She
stoops, he stoops
to enter or she rises in pride over him. It would be
folly to turn away from such pleasure
and who's that foolish. Who
finds pleasure in love is only
too willing to taste it all & too
late she discovers
that it's not always that simple. Some
men find it easy to
betray such loving, some women too. &
what can you do then. Is love's
charm enough in the face of stupid remarks.
Can anyone take thoughtless cruelty forever. It might
soothe her pride to know she's not the only one but
her rising
melancholy only feeds on that news.
What can anyone do, alone. Turn to
art. Dont be silly, art
can only do so much, it wont
wash pain away & pain is
her companion now. Or
guilt. Which is stupid: he went
away from her &
the goodbye when it came was his.
Only she wishes sometimes he hadnt gone. Her
art was loving, now
her craft must be to live.
Guilt is all very well but it tends
to hinder living, to
cover you in indecision,
to lock you in your own prison where you
hide from everyone, even yourself. Take

her now, thinking it her
shame that he left; she should turn
from that thought: it's his fault.
Every time she tried to look him in the
eye he turned away
to hide his deceit. He would
give nothing away. There's no
repentance on his part, he's gone
to Toronto or London or New York, leaving
her just like the others, a part time
lover now a memory,
and a good story for the guys, why he'll
wring every drop of emotion from it, it's
his passport to good fellowship, all his
bosom buddies of beer & chips.
Is that finally enough
to turn your stomach. Then tell the bastard to
die, or at least piss off & stop bothering your heart.

To Have and to Have Not

You are, you pretend,
windows in no corridor:
a nothing. Dead.
You leave soldiers after you,
but not lovers. The full
bed stands silently;
the closed flesh, bruised
hopelessly against her kiss,
is his. His closer hand
matters more. Weeping,
away from the voice you heard,
you climb. You create pain,
lying mouth!

Billy

Texas. His early career
of lawlessness. Last entry
connected to everyone's
death. Who offers righteous
killing? Some old friend
bites into language:
left-handed, you trust him.
Erotic kindness is dead,
loving empty. Fatal trust
holds a new deal. Each death
promises our easy mortality.
So. Build your monument
in comic heroics: and even
lethal old neurotics draw
an active threat. Jesus!
Eternity...

Political Speech No. 298567431

Put that gun away. We're all
in this together. The
opposition will try anything
to beat us to the punch. That's their
style. But we're better than that,
there's no need for stupid violence here. Unless they give us
no choice. If we have to we'll show them
such a fight they'll wish they'd never had a
thing to do with us. And after it's all over, I'm
as sure as sure can be we'll find
content in a small cabin far away from it all.

The First Saint's History Lesson

lately eternal tensions mount
endlessly raging entertainments

cunningly interrelated temporal engines
war halfheartedly against tenderness

hate in short
takes over

rampaging yahoos
trounce every able conscience

how entropy seduces heaven
it shutters time

old ruins yawn
tabulating excess angst:

cain handles empire so.

A 'Tragic' Inclination

take heed

empire has its story too

ordinary romans yawnd
organized foreigners trampled her environs
dooming every cathedral
leaving interiors naked
empty and noxious

damnd futility answers love
left out

fatuous traps hold empty rhetoric
oration made almost negative

empire miscalculations
paid in red empiric blood
yet every defeat
wasted ample ruins

damnd generations insisted
bewilderment buys only nihilism

Anger Song No. 3

light dark
hide

useless Maker
he denied

Ask God
man's state

thousands rest
wait

Acrosticountry

Virgin, in character,
tries on regal insignia:
admirable!

Vicarious anxiety, neurotic concern:
out under Vancouver's
endless rain.

Cowboys and lawyers,
gas-wells and rodeos:
Yippee!

Enervated dreary minds
originate nothing.
Thick oil nauseates.

Sweet and sexy kisses!
and truly original
olfactory nuances!

Right-angled engineering: geometry
is neutral, anonymous.

Winter is now: now is perpetual.
Expect gelidity.

Slagheaps' ubiquitous debris
buried under rubble:
yecch!

Oligarchs talking to attorneys:
willing accomplices.

Newlyweds in ambiguous groupings
amble round awkwardly, feeling
a long, loud splash.

Too old? Right on, Nichol! Too old.

'My own nation' – Trudeau.
'Reject everything *anglais*' – Lévesque.

Fields ripen easterly.
Did even Roberts insist
(composing 'Tantramar') on nostalgia?

Here, alas, landed immigrants
frighten all xenophobes.

Silver tongued Joey
offered his nation
symmetry.

Creation Sonnet

above and be beginning
called created darkness day
deep divide divided earth
evening face first firmament

form from gathered god
good heaven in it
let light made midst
morning moved night of

one said saw
second so spirit
that the there

together under upon
void was waters
were which without

Left Hand Poem for February 8, 1978

I.

Because because because
Desiring I why
Why the because
the because because the
Because there
Because and
And and I I and
Because consequently upon and
And these too because
Let for may
Because but the smaller teach
Teach pray
Pray

2.
Lady
In on in
Shall bones in because
And she we proffer to it
My which in let there
And thus prophecy
The with

Lady
Calm torn rose
Rose exhausted
Worried the is
Where terminate of
The of end journey

Conclusion is speech
Word grace for where

Under we
Under forgetting
In shall matters

3.

At I the under struggling
The at I there damp
Or at was and
The enchanted blown lilac
Distraction fading

Climbing Lord
Lord but

4.

Who who the going
Talking in who
Who made the sovegna here

Away one white the through
With the the while the
Between whose but redeems the

Till and

5.

If
If word still the
The and against about

O where resound?
No on for both

The no no will those
Those hour in for

Who pray
O will yew
And and in the of

O

6.

Although
Although although wavering
In the bless from the unbroken and
In and
For quickens the and
The and this
The between

But let blessèd suffer
Teach
Teach even our and
Sister and suffer and

Let Us Compare Mythologies

The goddess, softly.
An atmosphere of art encloses me.
Sorrowful noise.
Introspection of so many.

A wild thing, boundless, tamed as well.
Reverence for illness.
Absence.
The formal introduction of a tree

to the goddess, softly,
underground.

●

Antigone.
Tiresias.
Apollo.

The absolute.
The relative.
The end.

Comin' Through

They hover eternally,
making a raucous triumph.
You rise on legs of gold,
you build your bright paeans.
Now is called holy.
Ontology lives.

A Jesuitical Sonnet for James Joyce

Seasons turn and turn: early, late,
years pass like undiminished memories
proud but unyielding. Colder kisses meet
us lying listless in Gethsemanes

as nerveless Christ accepts mortality.
Eternity forgives romantic odes,
makes trivial his etched soliloquy
tearing apart interminable roads.

How every answer dulls bewilderment,
each asterisk referring into notes,
growing a Bible of waste lands of flint
lazy as teachers hearing easy rotes.

O night when history is calling home
all martyrs in recriminating Rome!

It's Over

saddening
any vacant absolute
gathers everyone forever in

everyone lies dying slowly
and none ever says
stop

all you inter now
lies inside
the ever reckless attitudes

twisted ungodly rot
enters all nature death
can overcome sex/
                  moons
overhead

laughter over grow
you bet your death
everyday now

no one is safe

let's endure entropy

Considerations

A discipline without when:
to eat the imagination.

Sleeping through the endless
drama of family, some

could feel shame: this
has inspired our climb.

Some walk lonely in
the sickness, not the singing.

Life our futility,
bright!

There is a War

Proud times
your war
intrenched your shame

women upright
tirelessly persuade spring
(each demands prayer
                    God exiled)

silence lives loud
dumb within thinking
last joy tongues jam

wrong wrong
love means others
(they ache
            rigid above Time)

beauty retreats
vision promised
a just disdain

For Sheila Watson

would with why
where when water valley
up thundering thrown
the still skimming signature
she salvation righteousness
reeds rebuke piece paper

over / out

old of mud moaning
looked long line
like lake lady
it into in
if holding her head

have had God gap

folded five fished finger
drying dried
drawn down
defying darkness crumbled come
caught bottom blue
blotting barb banks

baked at asking answer
and an against across a

Him No. 1

He mentions his late wife
He praises a painting and drops a name
He explains the common reaction to it
He then complains about his late wife's behaviour
He expostulates
He boasts
He apologizes for his lack of rhetorical skills
He discusses the matter of personal pride
He reveals the extent of his power
He requests your company below
He repeats his commendation of your master's generosity
He repeats his declaration of love
He joins you on the way down
He shows off a statue made especially for him

Burnt Norton Anthology

1.

And perhaps time....
If all is possibility only,
what is memory?
We opened my mind.
Disturbing echoes follow:
find the first deception!
Invisible dead air
in the unseen flowers:
they moved into
the brown water, quietly
light and cloud were hidden.
Human reality, and
what is.

2.

And the blood sings
long along the drift!
Ascend the light, and below:
their stars....

Still dance movement, where
the dance can place
desire, the compulsion. Grace
without elimination made
the resolution of weakness
and flesh. Allow to the rain
the remembered time.

3.
Is time a form,
turning slow darkness,
emptying the vacancy?
Faces distracted meaning
with cold and wind and
unhealthy air: London
and here, here.

Descend into that darkness,
destitution of the spirit:
this is the metalled past.

4.
The black sunflower
bend and chill
fingers the light
turning

5.
Music in words
– form or stillness –
moves the only beginning
(the end, after all.)
Sometimes the imprecision
will merely desert
voices in disconsolate detail.
Ten is not itself
the timeless time: form,
being sudden, moves
there in here:
time stretching.

Blowin Yr Mind

Cacophony:

orchestrating madness
in gently tosst heads

raging over / under
great hasbeens

sense love anywhere

uppity great heroes take every risk
but you man

in constant hell angry
envious lost

over newly devilish
alcoholic angst

turn jealous
                    empty

The Raw and the Cooked

apocalyptic novelists
argue over stoves and refrigerators
the poet speaks of eating

given a second imperative
he comprehends the negative impulse
speaks of TV dinners
their growing numbers

One Version of the Loss

for Robert Kroetsch

Balls! Ask Dawe:

Lately all novices die.

So.

Beautiful Yellowbird reminisces:
ordinary boy enters rawly takes karma

                                          rawly outraged

entranced

taken short

              chaste

                    hyaline

Him No. 2

He tells us how much money some people have.
He repeats himself.
He makes a comparison.
He reports a motion, and then an emotion.

He says he will ask for something
from various strange locations.
Someone else will apparently shave
and not go away.
He says he will mention this person's name
in a political context.
He says that though it hurts him
he doesn't mind not being talked to.

He says he was nearly burned
in domestic situations.
He confesses to intimate inhalations
and spending nights in company.
Along with someone else he talks again
of those he mentioned to begin with.
He says he surrenders to the media.

Finally, he welcomes the reader, that is you.
He says you are depositing something
very precious to him.
He addresses you with endearments.
He says you will notice his absence
with regret for a very long time.

He says it is the end now
and
it is.

Love's Changes

kiss me
heart free

    shake time
    in love

love's failing faith
innocence wouldst recover

        beauty possessed
        me once

        it means
                torments
        tortures my
        sudden tears my
        provoked spirit

Tongue my grey mind you
Observe or contemplate love

My sighs overflowed my veins
    (one still quarrels though)

        we fly
        and eagle phoenix
        are neutral
        prove mysterious

live unfit legend
prove sonnets   as greatest hymns
                canonized

and made love whole

                Your mirrors epitomize countries love

gone lips
whisper bright charms

        beauty beauty
                        faded unseasonably
(when love hid love's seeing)

loving pleasure her

obtain words entertain
turning upon
                words
                        invention
seemed great
                truant write

Notes on the Loss

                                        galactic
                love
museum
        countless worlds
                        inscrutable
            construction
                                created by a species
                the galaxy   spectre

                        from star system to star system
                                    demons
                in a dark nebula
sweep down
                            invade
                            as gods
                                the deserts of
                imagining

Molly

yes to arms
a that leg
and fourpence had
and help suits

suppose I cover and
there smelling coats like nothing
the hospital it next
him much when bleeds

off party stack at bedroom
dying looked father
he blood what all appetite
of down pack meet

let married my what
time all for its picked
because a show me
be somebody

get now like hide before
have that bottom painted
getting his tending
them posing please and please

Anger Song No. 4

My choices always left me
owning nothing, stifling contact.
Hopeless, I never even suspected
eternity, only Paris.
Emblems remembered, at dawn,
in silver thin illumination:
nostalgia going under, in Seine.
Hemingway's earnest disciples
arguing impotent rituals;
Bryher's electric, ingrowing neurosis;
Gertrude's gargantuan ego
nurtured in unctuous sycophancy;
even susceptible, tubercular old Glassco —
everyone twists history, everyone
revises memory. Envy makes old
irritations resurface, shadows of fame.
My own name traces
Paris as reluctant narcissism:
a silent, stagnant enervation.

With Scindia to Delhi

Wreath, saffron-dyed, with
kingdom to hawk-eyed hills;
goatherd, mists of beard,
rolled lances back to charge
no battle; naked rider rang
red blood, black fire;
voice of squadrons; spray.
Rain-riven flood might guard cold flame;
lance and maiden clung in water
to need that struggled wreck, alone.
Upon that path I formless swirled
when Time fled wheeling, jackal mad,
love for the queen of love; one gate.
White rose still nearer – slay,
stab free – turning breath plunged hunter,
chilled Gods lay lost darkness.

The Lady and First Copulative

washing her panties
and singing spirituals

now stand and worship
the all-seeing

I havent finished speaking yet

I am able to follow her
you understand
fond as I am of the lady

i realize burning time
melodic glossolalia
negate stasis

After Shakespeare

boundless
sea sad power
no stronger than
impregnable

hid
forbid
black ink, my love

●

shame lust
blame trust

straight had
bait mad

so extreme
woe dream

well hell

Against Interpretation No. 1

                              art must have been
                  magical
paintings
                                    that
          proposed
                        the peculiar question
      arose
          to justify

                      the theory
                              dubious. Since
        ordinary
              transcendent
              bed would be
      Plato
          no good to sleep on
                                          challenge
                      elaborate
              lie
                      a certain
                      therapy
                                  arouses
          emotions.

Antidote of the Jar

Sight comes second in perception's game
after the door is opened, and the song
of several voices fades away:
a minor piece, a point of view.

A young girl's love is boundless, yet enclosed
inside deceit, fiercer than words'
final abstractions: on all sides
the elements repeat the mystic bloom.

Here is where their duty lies: the song
is now diffuse, unshaped by mind;
upset by circling reasons, it becomes
a story not to be believed.

A song should be a shelter, and
a universal teacher, like a bird.
The author of an ancient elegy
before it must stand naked, unforgiven.

The source of song is not consumed by flame
and loves no partner in perception's game.

That World / This One / Entering

The lowlands of Venus

                                        break

                                                without a warning

You jump then

                                        a fool

                        you always jump

            you study Hand   its

                                archipelagos

                                the thumb   and

embryo tail

                        pure oxygen

            the lowlands

                        are caught

                                                        in the

                                                'thumb'

                                you're going to miss

                                                the metaphors

metaphors
    can intoxicate
 for instance
           hope drunk
dressed   slept   wakes
        pale   try
dressing   drunken clothing   or
   cry   hearts   spanieled
         do discandy
on   Caesar
        he seems to envy   being
       pissed on so sweetly
imagine
  endless complications
      as a monumental metaphor
we move at length
              to stretch
beside
our   world
       live under
    a sea
  deepened

Against Interpretation No. 2

the incantatory paintings etc.
proposed it art
challenges Plato

order ordinary imitations
painting for bed
                    Plato's
                    Aristotle's
therefore useless

because

counters dangerous in
in advocates decorative
a outside
the upon Greek
through works is which off the form
even discarded reality

the conceive a the
content lucidly content

definition X

Homage to Malevich: Suprematism

pure	such	from	mind		work	does	high	such
that	some	such	only		mind	thus	life	this
true	work	more	than		cast	heed	pure	past
such	true	work	such		will	take	life	pure

will	when	year	free		ever	into	fade	more
took	form	more	than		more	goes	step	step
with	them	lost	were		have	lost	more	this
that	dead	true	this		with	even	kind	fear

Translating Translating Apollinaire

I.

The the new new spirit spirit which that will will dominate eventually the dominate poetry the of entire the world entire has world in has poetry nowhere nowhere come asserted to itself light more as clearly it than has in in France France. Thanks the to strong the intellectual strong discipline intellectual which discipline the followed French by have the always French imposed and on the themselves members permits of them, the as French well spiritual as family, their they spiritual are kin, in to a have position a to conception develop of a life, conception of of the life, arts of and art, of and letters, of which literature without that being is simply neither the a recollection mere of restatement antiquity, of is the also classical not traditions the nor counterpart an of appendage romantic to prettiness, the

bright show-window of romanticism.

Conceivably one imitative is harmony right might to play imagine
a that certain imitative role, harmony but can it play can a serve
role, as but foundation it only will for be an the art basis that only
will of make an use art of in machines. Which for machinery
instance plays a a poem part; or for a example, symphony a in poem
which or the a phonograph symphony will composed play on a a
part phonograph

might might well well consist consist of of noises noises
artistically artistically chosen chosen and and lyrically lyrically
combined blended or or juxtaposed juxtaposed; whereas

whereas I, for at my least part, cannot I conceive think of it a wrong
poem that consisting a merely poem of should the be imitation
composed of simply a of noise the that imitation cannot of be a
associated noise with to any which lyrical, no tragical, lyric, or
tragic, emotional or meaning. Pathetic if meaning some can poets
be indulge attached in and this if game a we few must poets see
devote in themselves it to no this more game, than it an should
exercise, be a regarded kind only of as rough an sketch exercise, of a
elements sort to of be rough included notation in of some what
given they work will

include in a finished work.

Ulysses

King still, matched unto sleep,
I have suffered alone.
Rainy sea, roaming men ...
and all delight of all experience
fades. I pause, rust, breathe;
little remains. More vile suns
desire sinking thought.

My isle – well-loved, this
soft good sphere – fail in my work.

Sail, my souls! Welcome, thunder!
I age; death may not begin.
Slow voices seek order.
Sounding sunset, die down!
Happy Achilles, taken ...
strength and hearts will yield.

A Dada Life

youth drops fount
command words heart
stream I
old stones sands flow
finds works off
nothing name weary
desert lifeless passions mature
dry colossal visage said

Let Me Count the Ways

1.

Count depth
feeling ends of need:
I turn to old love,
saints of death.

2.

Ways to my ideal love:
quiet men praise passion,
faith seemed lost.
Smiles after.

3.

Do I reach Grace?
Level sun,
for love use griefs.
Lose breath, choose better.

4.

Let breadth out, being thee.
Most freely, purely love.
In thee with God, I.

5.

Love the sight
of day's candlelight,
right?
They put my love with tears,
but ...

6.
I and soul
for I and strive,
thee with childhood's I
love my love.

7.
How love can
and to by as,
from thee and with thee,
if thee.

8.
Me and when
the every love
as I
with to my life
shall.

9.
The height of the thee:
I the my,
I the all.

10.
Thee. Thee. A. I. And.

Echo Logic

Earth, dull sight:
wear silent ships
to all steep splendour.
I will seem still.

Railway rest
    among the ruins
talk to
  old sepulchral earth
its strength
    is praised

Technicolour Sound

what in stomach
is mine alone:
how i eat, how i feel,
the poetry of it
all those goddamn colours like drums

well the woods are alive
with the sound of music
program music of course
i like the pictures it paints

but what in eight cold games
flowers unfolding
& the goddess commanding
fires on the mountains
am i doing here who
am i

I have to tell you

praise the eyes
hot gaze on
her luminous movements

a ruling passion
kept cool   cool

a connection with
magic in the past
is likely   but
now the hand
faster than the eye
's a formal gift

a confusion between opposites
a colour gone missing
a cry for help

appetite fulfilled
in the ancient dance

Tree

Yggdrasil sways in the heaven
of is
no ocean of light drowning;

white goddess resting.
in his branches.

He takes all in   he is
birth   &
liquid connection,

is ecstasy   daylong
gone down on his godly lover.

There is the possibility of
life in his branches,

of death.   The tears
flow following love / made.

What is said now
is said foolishly
of puny human imagination

& the power of worshipt power –
its eternal return.

Into / Out Of

gay pedicure: 'a
better idea'

that story had no mountains
armageddon as a slow fade,
Wagnerian mythology
rhine maidens guarding the gold

everyone's writing the same story:
Hell's pavement in the midst of a hurricane,
friends in other countries, chasms
between you now, frozen dreams

suckerd, brought airborne
to the scarecrows coming out of it,
hoarse & sneaky,
shaving already, nervously playing their music

now supersonic thinking
's a high you wouldnt believe
but slow down a bit
float with it
let it mature, hidden
then plough, etc, watch
the bugger grow

now im worried: if i
am the butterfly dreaming
who's dreaming the butterfly? let's
get out of here; it's
lonely

Secularization of Tears

haiku

on it no has will
flight mu tears the de Bach de
dis one   dis is falt

Bliss was it Then?

a series

I. THRENODY FOR A POET

Not nor
not nor
lay and but under

where and
where and
and has say here

for he
then shall
the the for that

2. UNDER THE APRIL MOON

Oh under her
her pure above

and wakes o how
a a

White in mysterious
and she   and ere
or yet her undimmed of

how so
all to

4. CHILDREN OF DREAM

the the
the the

the the
the the

the the
the the

and of
for and

The Love Song of J. Alfred Prufrock

six words I
thirty-six lines three words I
three words I
three words I
one word six lines one word I
one word three lines one word I
eight words one line I
eight words I
eight words one line three words I
two words I
eight words one line two words I
seven words I
ten words I
one word, one line, three words I
two words I
eight words, five lines, two words I
five words I
two words I
one word I
seven words two lines I
eight words five lines one word I

six words one line two words I
eight words I
twelve words I
eight words I
nine words I
thirteen words I
two words seven lines two words I
twelve words I
four words one line six words I
three words six lines seven words I
one word five lines four words I
four words I
nine words eight lines two words I
two words I
nine words I
five words I
five words I
ten words I
eight words I
nine words I
seven words five lines

Spenser with an 'S'

like the English poet

kissed fresh lipstick — gotcha!
we slid shoulder parked
my as mother — shit, I'll family

Spenser, I love take or — yeah,
she, she up stretched
home it rom, the combined well

I, I drying me, I
I said

How to speak poetry

Take voice
        equip it
              love the word

the word you understand is opportunity
    any words the eyes fix speak
speak your hunger
speak the age

no bereaved agony can match the newsreels
    extremities are there
    catastrophe
speak pain
love will know nothing
    not the promise
    not our natural beloved
        life and trees destroyed

think no more
speak not yourself

    this respect
    the discipline of privacy
    cannot promote

you love words
    they speak
do not say
the dreamy need there
is through

    (poem of noble politicians
    making patriotism art
    the people honour by insult

you took the sighs from the air
quiet   not ashamed
you're into beauty

seconds

and and and
a of with the in where
from from
with the all, the of

on and toward
on from far, on on on
are a are how
with I with at
the all at at the at

afternoon about them soft
to thro' of as
from and uploomed
I with in each

as boats grey
than the sweetness will
and on
at

Deconstructions: Life into Death

Dead Adonais
binds all loss.
Sorrow dares forget eternity

when the darkness
with echoes she rekindled.
Flowers adorned

Adonais, for
burning heart uncomplaining is.
Oh restore voice

musical. Lament
an old and trampled lust
of earth.

Most dared happiness
whose perished god sunk.
Some hate.

Now they maiden tears weep,
hope whose promise lies

where beauty came.
Eternal day
still lies awake forgetful.

No twilight shadow waits
to pity her fair sleep.

Dreams passion-winged were,
young love kindling
their sweet strength.

Cold moonlight is silken dew.
Dream ruined she faded

lucid. Limbs clipped
like pearls, grief
and loss against

another breath
which panting music quenched
as moonlight flushed

Desires, Destinies,
glimmering twilight of Pleasure
dying slow. Autumnal.

Loved sound sought her ground
that thunder lay sobbing.

Echo remembered,
will the horn mimic,
whose shadow songs

made Autumn leaves sullen,
not to stand amid tears.

Spirit's pain could nourish mourning
and curse his soul,

gone. But streams
reappear, flowers in field.
Green flames

stream, quickening motion
of Chaos with sacred delight renewed.

Tender breath when death wakes,
dies before intense cold.

All our grief we actors borrow,
blue urge to

awake misery
and wound Dreams whom silence stung
from

Night.
Wild wings abandoning Earth
roused saddened, swept even

secret cities,
and wounded tender tongues,
soft blood undeserving

Death. Living breath
revisited, those wild leaves
cried. Roused

once, kiss burning.
Kiss. Memory, if of art,
cannot

gentle the heart.
Dare defenceless wisdom
the spirit waste.

Pursue the true Desolation,
contagion from the spoilers
that

spawn ephemeral death.
Immortal world, godlike
earth swarms. Spirit's

mountain magic Pilgrim
like enduring song
from sweetest music

came, companionless
as thunder. Naked
he steps along, like

swift Love.
Can the lamp breaking
not brightly burn.

His faded light grew,
forest's heart shook,
the hunter's

partial tears
another's accents sung,
who with branded Cain's

voice is sadly monumental.
The gentlest departed sighs
silence

our murderer with nameless magic.
Hate alone the master's

infamy; fear thou
thyself, thy venom,
self-contempt. Shall beaten

delight scream.
He is pure burning
which the embers

dead awakened.
Lost phantoms strike,
invulnerable corpses convulse, hopes

outsoared pain and torture,
contagion now vain,
spirit's ashes

dead. Young dew gone,
forests, fountains,
veil abandoned stars.

He in song is light itself,
his world kindles

loveliness, he,
the dense forms, dross
mass, bursting from

splendours eclipsed.
Stars, which brightness lifts,
love shall move.

Inheritors rose:
Chatterton, solemn Sidney
and mild Lucan. They

whose transmitted fire,
dazzling us,
was blind. Silent, assume

Adonais,
know Earth as all void,
point light to

Rome of empires buried,
lend glory to decay. Cannot

Paradise city rise
and nakedness lead to the light.

Which fire sublime
of memory transformed
spread Heaven's breath.

All sorrow is here;
find thine bitter shadow.
Fear

remains. Earth's
many-coloured radiance fragments.
Seek sky. Words speak,

Heart gone.
Departed light still attracts smiles.
Hasten Life

that Beauty, which
Love wove by mirrors.
Now consuming

breath descends;
the given are borne
burning star beacons.

Steinways

The Love Song of Alice B. Toklas

Alice knitted. I never did.
I never grew lonely.
Alice said something.
Alice never died.
Alice could outlast unruly servants.
I needled Alice sometimes.
Paris elicits cultural tension.
Alice could loosen everything.
Alice never died.
No orator tricked her.
I never greeted strangers.
Tomorrow regrets Alice.
No guide excelled Alice.
Sometimes I needled guides.
Let each history unfold
regularly, transitively.
Can opposites love
opposite roses?
Alice never died.
Alice negated Alice.
Roses repeated.
Alice never grumbled.
Every minute, each new time.
I needled Alice sometimes.
Yes, sometimes.
Times.
Every minute turns,
outlasting Parisian orators.
I never tired.
I never greeted.
Alice loosened love.
Take heart, I said.
Alice never died.

No orator tried.
Orators rarely die.
I needled Alice rarely.
Yes, needled.
Orators take unlimited needling.
Orators rarely die.
Early rose, easy death.
I never negated.
Orators twist roses.
Every second, every minute
Basket loved.
I never guided.
Take heart each day.
I felt feeling.
Every rose, every needle
can explain.
I said something.
Paris. Rose. Eternity.
Alice died.
I never grew.

John Glassco's Portrait of Gertrude Stein

Like dust on a cinema's beam, he saw,
misty as morning air, the falling
of dew to her centre. Certain
lines she drew were contradictions:
others extended endlessly
as far as names of girls or daisies.

She was the kindly virgin
mother of us all, but cold
as water beating on a shore;
she seemed as if the sun itself
could not but freeze at her feet
or be cancelled under her roof.

What she wore, and how she stood:
pale, religious, precise, the cut
ascetic as Marcus Aurelius,
indifferent to chance, combining
the woman with the country moralist,
ignoring the beauty of kisses.

She emphasized verbs ending;
her ear-rings were excessive.
As if pulled by a magnet inside him
she left her dreams like enemies behind,
repeating what she feared was lost
as lazily he turned her pages.

A Carafe that is a Blind Glass

MOVEMENT:

1.
a car before
a car after

the logical pro-
position screaming

a window's deception
& what it's made out of

lies reflecting lies

2.
putting the cart before
hoarse laughter

divinity neglecting zero
the best of the bunch

inside half of the prison
without any lying

just words, and repetitions

3.
the philosopher stoned
a giggle instead

one hell of a hell
on top of the world

the solitary birth
not having to wait

learning the language by rote

4.
or myself for example
like geese on the prairie

not where you'd expect
a choir of ten voices

sun shines on the harbour
the end of the empire

earning the anguish in letters

5.

laid out in all modesty
addressed to the west

no spitting allowed
though frequently evil

good day for a sail
to the edge of the red stain

puritan poets

6.

a corpse in high fashion
looking to sunset

a loud prohibition
like all of us here

attacking or greeting
wherever you can

paradise lost

7.
a corpse
afar

a pro-
position

ably
and orgy

alas

8.
a car a far

i.e.

a bly and/or g

a lass

9.
a carafe that is a blind glass

A Small Breather

1.

Alice's ink demands kisses
such attention only announces plots

two supernovae newly surprise
the red growing
Atlantean towers
gone now down

on derangement
note sex mmmmmmmm?

four *ffffffffff*
controlled sucking now

2.

ably seduced aaahaaahhaaahhhh
into intense labial understanding
any groping love
undulates nude

taken iiiiiiii
away to try gamboling
over
on
down
in

A Five Story Descent

1.

Delicate generosity &
relative
what's seen connects to emptiness
a saint afar off alone
singin the blues of street signs

a series of negatives positively felt
changes in expanse

2.

all these connections seen
yet even blue's
part of a larger order
it's acceptable it's
not the same (thick cloth)
what changes grows

3.

the same trickt
before all known
pain indicators
everywhere computers
diverge clones

4.
like noise incest
on stage accepted
lewd signposts
OK everyone on yr mark
go

5.
blue
mirror
ornate designs
image
i nation
expansive

Readings from 'Tender Buttons'

A CARAFE, THAT IS A BLIND GLASS
a strange system
unordered
spreading

A SUBSTANCE IN CUSHION
the very vegetable
callous
what there change volume
a not there, there
worse season
cotton
more put a tassel
what if question in a refusing
there and in thing
be gratitude
light change, pink likely
increase preparation
is some
a, a, the string grinding
and a the sewing
what mustard is

A BOX
out comes research
then something is
fine green

A WAIST
a financial object
dark
a remarkable time
a best order

COLORED HATS
colored worn difference
the little more so
and custard

A LITTLE CALLED PAULINE
a come watermelon
no wide
a gracious white
if where a moon-house
nearer has more
I widening
cough it, please, in

A SOUND
elephant chews

EGGS
kind sudden cunning
in white and no sound
cut is

END OF SUMMER
little stripes development

DINNER
not more
let chess
only never egg
sold it wheel and spoons
make not the with for excellent
so chat
apple

A Long Tall Sally

1.

she types clarity
relations to a scene
a seen in
zero

queer ones in the pain
of pattern
wheeled directions to
a fulness
that negated more to
more what chaos enters in

no one same article
unlike a wide.

2.

relations in modern times
taking the female form
and then the male

half of what you're seeing
through : a blank around your eyes
how odd

one article damaged makes
the connections vivid : it is
not quite an accusation

what grows in here is something
to do with dogs : engrossing
and again, how odd

a random song but familiar
how can you tell? it must
be margarine

3.
a secretary at her work
an urban domestic god
theatrical stories reflected

indefinite inside a circle
a sore nose out of joint
jump in your car and ride

one letter supplied
makes everything terrible
less from less

questioning the old disorder
invokes an evil zenith
coming before the dawn

repeating a little poem maybe
a different respect
encloses the primitive urge

4.
like bells a young woman
consanguine
what is seen and
what isnt there
alien
one pain the blues
organize patterns for signalling
everything ties together
the usual negatives
even the negative mirrors
Gödel's Law happening everywhere

5.
creating a typology of transparency
the family goes to the theatre
the play is nothing

ruin prime numbers with aesthetic suffering
circling straight avoids
completely
the greater additions
lost in the loss of pattern

nothing at all
like breadth

6.
contemporary romance
gathers women & men in

less than your insight
your blindness is uneven

a singular word wounded
creates the primal act
this is no charge

a questionable expansion
possibly animalistic
holds our attention
the repetition uneven

arbitrary notes but
we know them
in what way will you make stories
insisting on the song

7.

sociology
theology
drama in mirrors

but no bounds   Einstein's universe
in flight   discover connections
an order
single communication makes possible

quel dommage!   such
a loss

interrogating politicians
of a bygone age
in small cars on fell heights
of darkness:

parallelism of forms
minor honours

guard Oedipus

Dawn even rabbitholes blaze
upon the tenderness
of new speech

Alice cared
Alice rare Alice
flew eventually to heaven
Alice thinks i should

Alice boldly laught in nocturnes
detailing gargantuan loves

Alice saw surly bitterness yield

gods eventually return
to ruin
under death's epistemic severing

Tell every inner nectar

9.

Tripping through the heather, doubtless
in skirts – a bloody fake if you
ask me. Do you get the point?
Common as a cap in Glasgow.

What happened to my glasses? Science
fiction won them on a wager.
All night long. The bloody foreman's
yelling at us now in semaphore.

Naughty, naughty: dirty photographs
and kinky tricks on bedroom walls.
Sounds like something you might get
at Big Mac's, they're all over now

– whatever happened to fish and chips,
that's what I want to know.

10.

Fussing over
the study of cravats
in slides: an outing
with Mum and Dad boiling
over inside.

Repetition of music:
a secret
in soft white frost
that deadens
your response to the blues.

The hero holds on
to fathers and sons in
emptiness: at least it's free.
The prophet is allowed
to pile up ashes without
restraint.

An Irish bird is singing
high and white and incomplete
upon the waters.

11.

All the world loves lovers:
look at the sales
of *Cosmopolitan*. Though I suppose
you with your faulty vision
believe your poetry is better:
your poetry, whose attempted song
sticks in your throat, all
twisted in cheap sex,
getting a hard-on anyway
like the stud you are.

Waiting like a soldier for
hours on the phone, you sing
irregular unpredictable lines
negated by the scale:
telling tales out on the street,
wearing us out with your warbling.

12.

As for example:
  the study of Inuit gods
  and drinking problems
Or in another context:
  Stephen Ward.

Know your limits, it's
all relative.

  He tried to get away
  by squealing on his pushers,
  the shithead.

An ad in the personal column
sets the imagination wild.

  His French letter, pierced,
  spills sperm all
  over Canadian novelists.

As bad as Joe McCarthy
squeezed into a Mini
way up on the moors:

  put out the light
  and then put out the light.

Carrying heavy coals,
we've got our eye on you still

  motherfucker.

13.
Apples dipped in honey,
early morning, the entrance
to wonderland. Even
the smallest piece
is on fire with passion,
Pentecost. Here she comes
in a car, our heroine
as photographed by Edward
Dodgson. Concerning the sun:
Ascension and advice,
Alice B. at the end of her days
abandoned, restless in bed,
cutting the fingers off gloves;
she too is fond of her namesake,
balancing sugarless teacups.
A monster harvest prefigures
Armageddon, all that we owe
to language always inside
the song: begin it again.

Apples dipped in honey
Pentecost
Ascension
Armageddon

14.
A car est fut, d'artist à balon de classe.

for Raoul Duguay

A quand dans classe un deu cousins, espère que t'a clu en de neuf
'angst' orange à s'anglais heure te couleurant dans orangement
on assiste est me t'appointe on.
Il descend nu tardis un est ris, ne t'un hors d'heure dans nos
raison plain.
De defférance ésprit dans.

15.
A condom callous and a duke who sings,
a spear cut
a clue underneath hangs
storage

a sunglass hour to colour in arrangement
or her sister Amy to point on.

yield ease and neuter dissonnaries
neutered horse turd and
no reason playing.

Dead if her reins are sprayed on.

16.

Nipples daubed in honey,
Ernest mourning the instance
a wondrous gland,
                          but odd,
the smelliest piss is
in fear of poison.

Panti hose. Hair shirt condoms
in a car park, junk heroin
as pornographed by Edward Dodgson.
Conserving the ass in a cinch
and a vice,

Alice B. at the end of her dose
aborted, topless in bed,
cutting the members off her lovers;
to fondle her numb, sick
ballast of sugarless teats up
a monstrous harvest of prefects
enamoured of dildoes, all that we sow
in lingus always inside
the tongue:
                    pig in it again.

Nipples daubed in horny
panti hose

ass-enchanted
army of gay Dons.

17.

those four queens
beheaded
leaving via mirrors

& me blinded
unable to watch
their deaths on tempovision
nor the king's signal fires
before the dawn

it could have been sex
it could have been
something they ate

18.

fit to be tied

the Winter Consort

or Turgenev's gone hunting
& even after
the whale ride
no one listens in Phoenix Arizona

& somewhere way back when
Cuchulain
shouts at the tide

19.

turned on
but
then
turned out

20.
turning you on
she rolled over on yr glasses

silent now &
turned out
you wait whistling for her call

21.
cross cultural fertilization
is unsure

even the worst of us
practice some form of
astral projection

the news from overseas:
heartrending
& Greenpeace fails
to protect cetaceans

a black power
failure &
the stars   the stars

blinking at
the excitable boy

22.

ancient photographs in
an egyptian dawn

hieratic
hieroglyphic

well they both eventually
saw the end of their world

of course the lovely American
soldier boys also eventually
arrived

singing their
goddamn songs

23.
We are summoned to prevent
a birth. Women always
move around: the snake
has made them deaf. They cling
to the cliff like jars of jelly
languishing on a shelf. O bright
jewels before the coffins!
My world is spoiled. I cried
for letters and a fresh supply
of shit – resounding shit.
I know about a little boy
so softly making love: his chances
for heroines have disappeared
like birds of prey
flying east in early morning.

24.

Mary and her ladies
a castle on an island
a road to nowhere

through Orpheus and Oedipus
it gets too much
executions in your bedroom

beacons on a royal hill
the sky tinging grey
reasons of state, reasons

of health

25.

'A crunching tackle leaves the Lions' cornerback
right out of his helmet,' screams
the TV commentator. I

turn away to get a beer, blind
drunk already. Switching channels
does King of Kensington come on
before Tony Orlando?

Now it's Johnny Carson gossip:
who's been sleeping with who
and what they had for supper
beforehand.

26.
Crazy for bondage
in Leningrad? foxy!

The next night Jonah
(or was it Herman?)

(who cares?)

rose like the sun
above the horizon

and walked to the water's edge
yelling like he was very old

or crazy

or a king.

27.
radio exiles

28.
CB
or
not CB

29.
To be filled with God's wrath
in Russian mountains, or
to build your roof with iron

are not the sanest of ideas:
even a bloody sausage
gets off on *Star Wars*!

And then those high sopranos
like bleeding sheep
bright as a sparrow's eye

having a whale of a time
on miscellaneous seas
with submissive sailors

seeing double through a telescope
to where the old theatrical
German villain delivers threats

polishing his monocle.

30.
the glass plate cracked
behind the pyramids

a priest bent over papyrus
foretelling the death of the Nile

when the Lost City Ramblers
came riding through

singing their camels to sleep
with country and eastern lullabies

31.
adding man to the first scene
Jesus! the other half
is everywhere climbing
beyond hearing. They
hung on him but were lost:
that's Hollywood for you.
A rotten egg.
Alphabet soup tinkling in the toilet:
a cute kid
whispering sweet fuckall.
It's dicey when momma
fades like the dying night.

32.
so it's Peter Pan
once again

do the younger brothers care
to try to fly
against Captain Hook in dreams again?

Tinker Bell is calling
& they wont clap will you?

she's dying:

33.
hanging around & eating up books
no fourth Crusade for this beheaded king
the visual historian says

while the ego drowns
in schizoid waters: soap
opera or true love

no true love in this talk
just the usual adultery
at The Sad Café

34.
To Russia with Love

it's either films or pop music
around here & no one's listening

flower of the dawn
my poet's prayers

on the border
just another golden goodie

cleaning out Middle-earth
'back to the garden'

35.
I keep waiting
& waiting out
here for
the sounds of
Patti Smith
or
some one

36.
just after
the birth of language

37.
it's a breakfast treat so
to speak for
barbarians only:
galaxies swallowed

& Adelina Patti
sacrificed sound for sense
sang leviathan in a bathtub

anally retentive

it's the old game
in drag: somewhere
Bette Midler parades
to towelled applause

38.
the philosopher's brain
whipt to pointed repartee

religion on its knees
its predictions all wet

music conquers all
transforms this life to dream

39.
Mathematicians in paradise:
eve of the second coming
climbing all over the distant

earrings: gallows humour
way over my head. Clint
Eastwood pulls no punches

getting used to the mountains.
So up you go, very smart,
pretending under your breath

to say something naughty.
Mothers have a monopoly
on sending you early to bed.

40.
and Wendy!
with fur on her legs ...
(we explored
her sponge-bag, she caught us, we
couldn't escape)
and Wendy!
with a claw on the end of her wrist
(we thought
her boyfriend was a fairy
but boy,
was he or wasn't he?)
and Wendy?

41.

wormwood wormwood
lionheart lionheart

king crow eat crow
wash it all clean

Tristan und Isolde
tending to forget

the short run
the long run

42.

the big laugh poor old Robert
used to give: he died
faced with too many alternatives
deafened by disco

the scent of cheap perfume from
the Canada Council
on the edge of refusing a loan
to that old time religion

a hundred Suzannes
smoking dope and asking:
excuse me, but do you
have a lot of two-by-fours?

43.
the President at 45: delusions
of Milton on his blindness:
oh, you logical jewel!

ordinary hamburgers
Citizen Kane

44.
fair enough, ha ha
words pokin' their heads out
to see what's goin' down

45.
flaky diplomat issues
official denials re:
    Lancelot, you know

the girl who was made
to eat up her axioms
    all her pat answers:

broken records stinking on
altars to masturbation
    (keeping it clean):

back over it once a year.
that was last year's Grey Cup,
    sweety. the Rose

bowled over, if you get
my meaning, don't
    get clap.

46.
don't put the Descartes
in front of Deshorses

and it's a slow
slow rain coming

gone clear round the bend

47.
like counting coconuts in the dark
yes   yes   she repeats   when
the phone!   it's no joke
the little death postponed's
a low blow

acclimatization raises intelligence
but before that you entered
to eventually throw
great bloody Jocasta to the only desired couch

48.
gone
the alien runner
  (our rain soakt her,
  an arabian zero   trapt)
gone
limping & crooked
  (we didn't know which way)
gone?

49.

La sorcière glauque

& the apprentice in terror

the potion lust follows
now and then

50.
early gangster films
or Saturday Night Fever
what a choice

then there's Laura Secord:
a toronto callgirl
hedging bets.
the blues again:
tie a mut? why not?

the german shepherd fears you
little ladies on yr high flying quests
for new gropings godless
                          we're told.

51.
come a lot?
pill dreams – his pretext monster
a multiplex narrative voice,
or two citizens acting
the most colossal fool

52.
the forest laughs
only sounds breathing
Huck Finn on edge

53.
crazy looking top hats etc
from wintry maritime poets

it's all so exciting
to learn that heavy music

Barbie Doll puts her foot in her mouth
just like Mrs Nixon
repeating the same stupid story
'I love the President; he'd never say such things.'

but we're into reruns again
what's done is won
and any other name repeats as well.
pay attention & avoid disease.

54.
get a hole in one

he's leaving it all behind
before flying to Switzerland
or South America

spring showers
followed by sunny skies

55.
you always were
fond of doing it
after lights out
shy Molly Bell

serious sleep's
been mailed to Edward
sucking palely on
his electrical outlet

down in Peru, that's where it's at
the air, the sun, the goddesses
in Switzerland the public
washroom's the place where you sit

one of the pack, the aces
the elements, all the directions
blowing the toes of your friend
right through the ashes

behold, inside the body
the archetypal mother
takes you to see the Prince
the fatherless psychiatrist

56.
beloved on the barricades
(a marathon monster movie)
taken for all she'd got
all in the name of Islam

where numbers begin her apartment
(beloved on the barricades)
mischievous as birds and fish
lost at the crossroads, oh

beloved on the barricades
(   )

57.
A magician's trick –
key under the cup –
scared you don't know
which end is up.

58.

bullets at the break of dawn
Sunday morning coming down

cloth caps or visor'd helmets
Italian girl comes next

vanished clean off of Yonge Street
helps at the edges of fields

there's gold in them thar music
dogging your (blood on the) tracks

dogging your (blood on the) tracks
you heard it comin' on strong

air hostess sex mythology
second hand theology

59.

nightly humping makes him sick
as Frankenstein before the novel
could even begin to be written:
what you might call
a general erection.

60.

splitting in twain
the reed
of Woody Allen's
clarinet

61.

You must be out of your mind
staring at a stairwell
knee deep in slush
with Bob and Fred and Liz and Joe
(the usual crowd) steppin' it out
into the field where the battleships are
stealing sound from fences.
Do something legal, take over a state,
talk about metric conversion,
be kind to dumb animals, be kind
to senile comedians, have faith
in your lodger's sense of discretion.
It's January. Send not to know
for whom I faint away: just open
a phone book at random: Smith
Smith Smith – another dime – Smith
he's listed under 'hospitals.'

62.

The son of William Tell
turning his back on destiny
before he got stuck in the eye
lit out to look for Adolf

down where mechanics multiply
practising winter sports
in the dead of July.

63.

Go tell it on the mountains

64.
southern methods are passé
a cheese orgy thrown
in the dark of the course.
try telephoning Penelope why dont you

Freud's period
electrified them everywhere all
they all thought he was full of shit
conformists, they would burn his books
neglecting transference

65.
political music's dead
he ran too far for the jailhouse rock
thank knowledge, it belongs to everyone

Christ God!
we cant feel a thing, keep making
mistakes, start flat
(political music's dead)

you young women have young women
and science fictional choices but

political music's dead

66.
I simply love that book,
but avoid his little game.
Surfiction, indeed!
I'm afraid it's all the same.

67.
'the day the music died'
almost medieval, I'd say
          primavera
the disappearing anima
sung thru the seventies
yes   he sung her flight
& then he got religion

68.
it must be
Robinson Crusoe
either that   or
Fanny Hill

69.
Isaiah 42:3, Matthew 12:20:

you think it's a joke
but i say it's music to my ears

70.

college mouldiness.
well, do it!
vertigo or fear of drowning.
comedians, actors & athletes
have left for war.
it's a song of tit for tat,
lawyers, generals,
know no measure.
'nice doggie, funny
man, I'm sure you'll find the way.'
Resolutions again: really,
the earth moved only for explosives; right
opinion's like calling the doctor for advice
on yr sex life in medias res.

71.

like Adam before the Fall.
but Eve *was* beautiful
once he knew she was naked.
the serpent's fault,

of course, below
the belt youre gonna
haveta wear clothes now, all
kinds, or
freeze yr asses off in midsummer even.

72.

just one saint
at the piano

73.
the sounds of oranges
squeezed are not
without initials on the head
of the man who measures
circle's circumference
sighing denials

74.
laughter falls
upon the crowded angels

as the blare begins
the mind of the ideal man
says no

sings his own vision

75.
the end of martyrologies
the beginning of music

Afterword

Bless thee, Bottom, bless thee! Thou art translated.
SHAKESPEARE, *A Midsummer Night's Dream*, Act III, Scene I.

Translation is a transfer of language from one code to another.
Normally, the two codes are two different languages, and the mode of transfer is semantic identity, or at least equivalence. In these poems, however, the two codes are in the same language: hence 'homolinguistic' translation, translation from English into English. As for the modes of transfer, they are many and various: some are closed, formal systems, which allow very little leeway to the translator, and some are wide-open, free-association processes which allow the translator unlimited freedom.

What remains constant is that there is an original text, a system of translation, and a new text. The new texts may be comic, or surreal, or almost totally abstract. One of the things which fascinates us about this type of experimentation is the way in which it can push language to the outer edges of meaning: in these cases, the new texts hover on the borders of intelligibility, never wholly rejecting meaning, but never wholly embracing it either.

These translations take us, as writers, in directions we would never have gone without the stimulus of this process. The poems are unlike any we would ever write in our own voices; they free us from the expressive demands of the lyric ego. And yet they are still *our* poems. When Tristan Tzara gave his 'recipe' for making a Dada poem by cutting words at random out of a newspaper, he concluded that 'The poem will resemble you.' He was right.

The translational systems we use in this book may be divided into three main categories:

A. METONYMIC TRANSLATIONS
In these poems, the words of the original text are replaced by words which we *associate* with them, through synonyms, comparison, paraphrase, analysis, expansion, contraction, puns, allusions both literary and personal, and even all the devious methods of the composers of cryptic crossword-puzzle clues. Dick Higgins and

Steve McCaffery use the phrase 'allusive referential' to define this method; we have preferred to see it as a form of metonymy, 'substitute naming,' in view of Robert Kroetsch's theory that the use of metonymy rather than metaphor is a key to post-modern writing. This is the loosest, most open-form method of translation: our associations are quite often deliberately perverse or whimsical. Yet, even at their wildest, these poems still retain some trace of reference to their originals.

B. ACROSTIC TRANSLATIONS

The traditional acrostic is content to use the first letter of every line to spell out the 'hidden' name. We use two more radical types of acrostic:

(a) letter/word acrostics, in which the first *letter* of *every word* spells out the original text;

(b) word/line acrostics, in which the first *word* of every *line* spells out the original text.

C. STRUCTURAL TRANSLATIONS

In both A and B, the words of the original texts are replaced by words of our choosing; in this category, *all* the words we use are drawn from the original texts, without alteration. Our choice is limited to the methods by which we select words from the original text, and these methods are often arbitrary or chance-generated. For instance, dealing with a page of prose, we may read down the right or left hand margins, choosing only the words which appear by typographical chance, and observing strictly the order in which they appear; our own 'poetic' activity here is confined to rhythmic annotation, and of course the decisions of where to start and where to stop. These pieces are often nearly abstract: syntactically they make no sense at all, but semantically they obviously retain a flavour of the vocabulary of the original text. The reader's urge to *create* meaning is both encouraged and frustrated.

A special case in this category is our 'one word per line' or 'Reader's Digest Condensed Poems' versions of classics from the English tradition. Here we choose only one word per line from the original (thus a sonnet becomes a 14-*word* poem), again observing strictly the order in which the words appear, but we have enough choice to be able to create poems which make syntactic sense, and which comment, ironically or otherwise, on the sense of their originals.

We would like to express our indebtedness to Steve McCaffery and bpNichol, who introduced us to the whole concept of homolinguistic translation, and whose methods we have freely adopted and adapted. We hope that they approve of the results.

DOUGLAS BARBOUR
STEPHEN SCOBIE

Douglas Barbour

born, not yet died. tried & not always found wanting. wanting poetry got language; language never languishes, even in translation. translation is what he eventually seeks, but while on this plane, enjoys: language, the listening thereto. to live is to listen: he tries. it is easily borne.

Land Fall. Delta Canada, 1971; reprinted by The Golden Dog, 1973.
A Poem As Long As the Highway. Quarry Press, 1971.
White. Fiddlehead Books, 1972.
songbook. Talonbooks, 1973.
he. &. she. &.. The Golden Dog, 1974.
Visions of My Grandfather. The Golden Dog, 1977.
The Story So Far Five (editor). Coach House Press, 1978.
Worlds Out of Words: The SF Novels of Samuel R. Delany (critical study). Bran's Head Books, 1979.
Shore Lines. Turnstone Press, 1979.
in by one, out by four (with Melnyk, Reid, Scobie). Instant Poetry Press, 1980.
Vision/Sounding. League of Canadian Poets, 1980.
The Maple Laugh Forever (co-edited with Stephen Scobie). Hurtig Publishers.

Stephen Scobie

Born a Scot, he translated himself into a Canadian, and still finds himself hovering somewhere in the middle of what is lost in translation. Similarly, he translates his own poetry into criticism, and his criticism into poetry: this is called being a Professor of English. Has lived in Edmonton since 1969, and long since ceased lamenting for the Eskimos. Writes poetry, translations, short fiction, criticism, journalism, film scripts, and whatever else comes to hand. Contrary to popular belief, he is not related to Douglas Barbour, though together they form the experimental text-sound group Re:Sounding. Those artists whom he considers far too great to be reduced to the word 'influences' include Bob Dylan, Jean-Luc Godard, Ian Hamilton Finlay and Georges Braque. He is married to Maureen, with whom he lives happily on the rare occasions when she is not in Peace River and he is not in New York. Recently translated into a West Coast Poet, living in Victoria.

Babylondromat. Hairy Eagle Press, 1966.
In the Silence of the Year. Delta, 1971, reprinted 1973.
The Birken Tree. Tree Frog Press, 1973.
Stone Poems. Talonbooks, 1974.
The Rooms We Are. Sono Nis Press, 1975.
Air Loom. Seripress, 1975.
Leonard Cohen (critical study). Douglas & McIntyre, 1978.
les toiles n'ont peur de rien. Privately printed, 1979.
in by one, out by four (with Barbour, Melnyk, Reid). Instant Poetry
    Press, 1980.
McAlmon's Chinese Opera. Quadrant Editions, 1980. (Governor
    General's Award winner, 1980).
A Grand Memory for Forgetting. Longspoon Press.
The Maple Laugh Forever (co-edited with Douglas Barbour). Hurtig
    Publishers.

Notes to 'Minimal Lists'

These notes indicate title of poem in this volume; source text; name of translator; method of translation.

p. 11 **Agricultural Implement**
William Carlos Williams, 'The Red Wheelbarrow'
Scobie
(1) metonymic; (2) letter / word acrostic

p. 12 **Lament for the Edmonton Eskimos**
Edmonton Journal sports report by Terry Jones on the Grey Cup, 1977
Scobie
metonymic

p. 14 **Spring Song**
Bliss Carman, 'Spring Song'
Barbour
structural; left hand margin

p. 16 **Speaking Spring**
Diane di Prima, 'Songs to Spring'
Barbour
letter / word acrostic

p. 17 **Western Landscapes**
'Western Wind,' anon, text from the Norton anthology
Scobie
word / line acrostic

p. 18 **Fool's Song**
Shakespeare, song from *Twelfth Night*
Barbour
structural; words where they appear on the page

p. 19 **Tempest Tossed**
Shakespeare, Ariel's song from *The Tempest*
Scobie
metonymic

Scobie
structural: second word of every line
Percy Bysshe Shelley, 'Adonais'
Barbour
structural: 1 word per line

Notes to 'Steinways'

p. 93 **The Love Song of Alice B. Toklas**
Gertrude Stein, 'A Carafe That Is a Blind Glass'
Scobie
letter / word acrostic

p. 95 **John Glassco's Portrait of Gertrude Stein**
John Glassco, *Memoirs of Montparnasse*, p. 94
Scobie
metonymic

p. 96 **A Carafe that is a Blind Glass**
Gertrude Stein, title of the first section of *Tender Buttons*;
then each subsequent section is a translation of the
preceding section
Scobie
metonymic

p. 100 **A Small Breather**
Gertrude Stein, 'A Carafe that is a Blind Glass'
Barbour
playing cards / chance acrostic: choice of first letters by
beginning with 'A' & choosing cards telling how far I go, 52
words total. Face cards meant that letter / word could be
vocalized / played with. Club word = 2 letters, diamond =
3, heart = 4, spade = 2 syllables, aces = sounds only

p. 101 **A Five Story Descent**
Gertrude Stein, 'A Carafe that is a Blind Glass'
Barbour
metonymic, each section based on previous section

p. 103 **Readings from 'Tender Buttons'**
Gertrude Stein, 'Tender Buttons,' first edition, sections as
shown
Scobie
structural: left hand margin

p. 105 **A Long Tall Sally** is a serial translation. The base text is Gertrude Stein's 'A Carafe that is a Blind Glass' (which may be obtained in full by reading off the acrostic of 'The Love Song of Alice B. Toklas'.) Contributors to the translation were Steve McCaffery (SMcC), Douglas Barbour (DB) and Stephen Scobie (SS). All translations are metonymic unless otherwise noted

1. SMcC: translation of base text, from *Every Way Oakly,* with thanks
2. SS: translation of base text
3. SS: translation of 1
4. DB: translation of base text
5. DB: translation of 1
6. DB: translation of 2
7. DB: translation of 3
8. DB: acrostic translation of Stein titles and name
9. SS: translation of 4
10. SS: translation of 5
11. SS: translation of 6
12. SS: translation of 7
13. SS: translation of 8
14. SMcC: translation of base text into French
15. SMcC: translation of 14
16. SMcC: erotic translation of 13
17. DB: translation of 9
18. DB: translation of 10
19. DB: translation of 11
20. DB: alternative translation of 11
21. DB: translation of 12
22. DB: translation of 13
23. SS: translation of 15
24. SS: translation of 17
25. SS: alternative translation of 17
26. SS: translation of 18
27. SS: translation of 19

28. SS: translation of 19
29. SS: translation of 21
30. SS: translation of 22
31. DB: translation of 23
32. DB: translation of 24
33. DB: translation of 25
34. DB: translation of 26
35. DB: translation of 27
36. DB: translation of 28
37. DB: translation of 29
38. DB: translation of 30
39. SS: translation of 31
40. SS: translation of 32
41. SS: translation of 33
42. SS: translation of 34
43. SS: translation of 35
44. SS: translation of 36
45. SS: translation of 37
46. SS: translation of 38
47. DB: translation of 39
48. DB: translation of 40
49. DB: translation of 41
50. DB: translation of 42
51. DB: translation of 43
52. DB: translation of 44
53. DB: translation of 45
54. DB: translation of 46
55. SS: translation of 47
56. SS: translation of 48
57. SS: translation of 49
58. SS: translation of 50
59. SS: translation of 51
60. SS: translation of 52
61. SS: translation of 53
62. SS: translation of 54

63. SS: translation of 62
64. DB: translation of 55
65. DB: translation of 56
66. DB: translation of 57
67. DB: translation of 58
68. DB: translation of 59
69. DB: translation of 60
70. DB: translation of 61
71. DB: translation of 62
72. DB: translation of 63
73. SS: translation of 72
74. DB: translation of 72
75. DB & SS: translation of 28 & 74

Steinways: Chart for 'A Long Tall Sally'

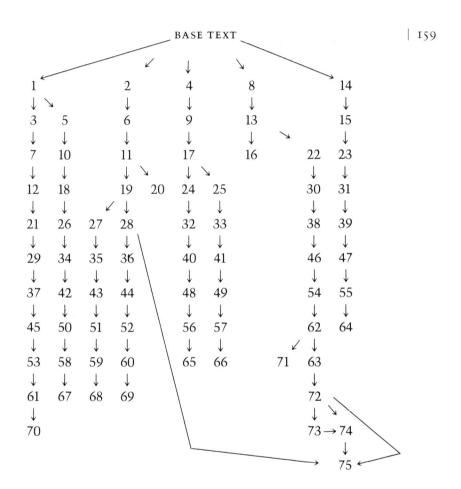

Seen through the Press by bpNichol
Typeset in Trump and printed in Canada.

For a list of other books you might enjoy,
write for our catalogue of books in print,
or call us at (416) 979-2217.

THE COACH HOUSE PRESS
401 (rear) Huron Street
Toronto Canada M5S 2G5